THE CHEYENNE

ARTHUR MYERS

THE CHEYENNE

Franklin Watts   New York   London   Toronto   Sydney   A First Book

This book is dedicated to
Virginia Ritchie Cutler

Map by Joe Le Monnier

Cover photograph copyright© The Smithsonian Institution,
Washington, D.C., (89-10230)

Photographs copyright ©: The Smithsonian Institution, Washington, D.C.: pp. 3 (89-10265),
24 top (89-10247), 24 bottom (89-10240), 43 (270-A); National Cowboy Hall of Fame, Okla-
homa City, OK.: p. 10; Sid Richardson Collection of Western Art, Ft. Worth, TX.: p. 13
(#SWR80, 1901, Charles M. Russell, "Returning to Camp"); Buffalo Bill Historical Center,
Cody, WY., 82414: pp. 17, 21; The Philbrook Museum of Art, Tulsa, OK.: pp. 18, 28, 29;
Western History Collections, University of Oklahoma: p. 23 top; American Museum of Nat-
ural History: 23 bottom (324004); The Thomas Gilcrease Institute of American History and
Art, Tulsa, OK.: p. 33; Woolaroc Museum, Bartlesville, OK.: pp. 36, 38, 39; Nawrocki Stock
Photo, Chicago, IL.: p. 37; North Wind Picture Archives: p. 44; John Warner Photography:
pp. 50, 51, 52, 53.

Library of Congress Cataloging-in-Publication Data

Myers, Arthur.
The Cheyenne / by Arthur Myers.
p.   cm. — (First books)
Includes bibliographical references and index.
Summary: Describes the history, customs and beliefs, and current
status of the Cheyenne Indians.
ISBN 0-531-20069-8
1. Cheyenne Indians—History—Juvenile literature.   2. Cheyenne
Indians—Social life and customs—Juvenile literature.
[1. Cheyenne Indians.   2. Indians of North America.]   I. Title.
II. Series.
E99.C53M93   1992
970.004'973—dc20   91-31010 CIP AC

CONTENTS

THE CHEYENNE

HOW THE CHEYENNE BECAME HUNTERS AND FIGHTERS

The Cheyenne were one of the most feared, yet one of the most admired, Indian tribes during the time of the white man's expansion across North America in the 1800s. They were never a large tribe in numbers, but when settlers and U.S. troops began to flood across their lands, the Cheyenne fought back with skill, cunning, and often ferocity. They were a tall, athletic, and handsome people. They had an appreciation of themselves—calling themselves *Tsistsistas,* which in their language means "the beautiful people."

The Cheyenne are remembered largely as horse-mounted Indians of the Western plains—as stalking the great herds of *buffalo,* swooping down on settlers whom they saw as invaders of their land, and massing in war

A CHEYENNE BUCK STUDIES THE
LANDSCAPE IN THIS FREDERIC
REMINGTON PAINTING.

parties against other tribes and U.S. soldiers. They were *nomads,* constantly on the move across the wide *prairie,* setting up their buffalo-hide *tipis* and tearing them down when the hunting became better elsewhere. But when they first met white people, some three hundred years ago, the Cheyenne were living in a different sort of place, leading a life quite unlike that of the roving, sometimes fierce Plains Indians they later became.

The Cheyenne, like other Native Americans, first came to North America from Asia about fifteen to forty thousand years ago. They encountered whites for the first time in 1680, when the Cheyenne were living in what is now Minnesota. A group of Cheyenne visited the fort of the French explorer *La Salle.* At the time, the Cheyenne lived in permanent villages of large *lodges* made of packed earth. They hunted small *game* and gathered fruits and plants. They relied on farming for most of their food, sowing crops of corn, beans, and squash. They were skilled makers of pottery. But around 1700 they were forced westward to the Missouri River by the Sioux tribe. The Sioux had acquired guns from white traders. With these weapons, they were able to force their will on the Cheyenne, who were still using spears and bows and arrows. The Sioux themselves were being crowded by white settlers and the Chippewa, and before long they too would be forced to move onto the Western plains. Their lives would also radically change. Even-

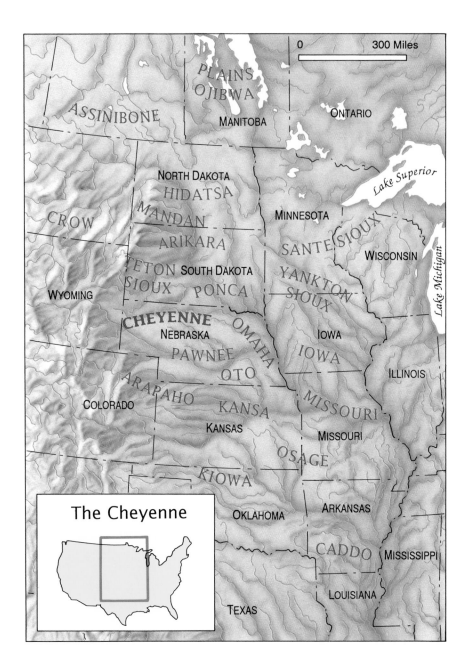

0   300 Miles

PLAINS OJIBWA

ASSINIBONE

MANITOBA

ONTARIO

Lake Superior

NORTH DAKOTA

HIDATSA

MANDAN

ARIKARA

CROW

MINNESOTA

SANTE SIOUX

WISCONSIN

Lake Michigan

TETON
SIOUX

SOUTH DAKOTA

YANKTON
SIOUX

WYOMING

PONCA

CHEYENNE

NEBRASKA

OMAHA

IOWA

IOWA

PAWNEE

OTO

ILLINOIS

ARAPAHO

MISSOURI

COLORADO

KANSA

KANSAS

MISSOURI

OSAGE

MISSOURI

KIOWA

The Cheyenne

OKLAHOMA

ARKANSAS

CADDO

MISSISSIPPI

LOUISIANA

TEXAS

MEMBERS OF A CHEYENNE TRIBE
START TO RETURN TO THEIR CAMP
AFTER A SUCCESSFUL HUNT.

tually, the Sioux became allies of the Cheyenne against the Crow, Pawnee, and others.

In their new home along the Missouri River, the Cheyenne were still under pressure from the marauding Sioux. But in the late 1700s something new entered their lives—the horse. The horse had been introduced to North America by the *Spanish conquistadores,* and its use had gradually worked northward and eastward. New opportunities opened for the Cheyenne when they began to acquire horses.

The plains to the west were teeming with buffalo and *antelope.* These large, fleet-footed animals were very difficult to hunt on foot, but not on horseback. To escape the Sioux, the Cheyenne moved out onto the plains. They gave up farming. As the later Cheyenne put it, "We lost the corn." They stopped making pottery; it was too easily broken in their new life of constant moves. Guns now became an important part of their lives, and they became the hunting, fighting, roving people that history recalls so vividly as the Cheyenne Indians.

CHEYENNE BOYS AND GIRLS PLAYED HARD AT BECOMING MEN AND WOMEN

Men and women had sharply different roles in the Cheyenne way of life. The men were aggressive hunters and fighters. The woman ruled over the life of the tipi—cooking; gathering wood, water, and berries; and making robes, moccasins, and other articles of clothing. Boys and girls began to learn adult activities, and practiced them at a very young age. Boys began learning to ride almost as soon as they could walk, girls soon after. By the time they were five or six, the boys were riding bareback on their own *colts* and mastering the use of the *lasso*. By seven or eight, they were helping with the herding of the camp's horses.

The boys were given small bows and arrows as soon as they could learn to use them. In their playing at hunting, they learned caution and patience. They would creep through the brush, taking advantage of all possible cover. They stalked small game, but in a few years they would be hunting buffalo and antelope.

The boys joined with the girls in "play camps." The girls had small tipis, made for them by their mothers. The children mimicked family life throughout the day. The girls learned child care. They did beadwork and quillwork. They learned to cook wild roots, such as the bulbs of lilies and the red turnip. They collected berries such as chokecherries, ground them, and mixed them with dried meats. In the mornings, they would go out from the camp and dig roots. Sometimes, when the work became tiresome, they would pretend they were a war party and give out war whoops. Boys, joining in the game, would charge out from the camp and the girls would await them with sticks and chips of dry buffalo manure. A boy who was hit with such missiles would be considered wounded and out of the game.

The boys would try to catch fish and shoot birds and rabbits for the families' food. The boys were too young to hunt real buffalo, but they learned to hunt with some of the boys acting as make-believe buffalo. They would carry a *prickly pear* on a stick to represent the buffalo's horns and heart, and then go out to *graze*. The other boys would mount sticks and "ride" out to surround the "buffalo." The hunters would shoot blunt arrows at their prey. The rules of the game were that if

CHEYENNE GIRLS WOULD
PRETEND TO BE MOTHERS—
PRACTICING FOR THE TIME
WHEN THEY WOULD USE
CRADLEBOARDS LIKE THIS ONE
FOR THEIR OWN BABIES.

an arrow went through the center of the pear, the "buffalo" was considered to have been brought down. But if the arrow was off center, the bull was only wounded. Then the "buffalo" could turn on the hunter and swat him in the rear with the spiny prickly pear.

The children also played war. The girls would dismantle the tipis of the play camp and flee with their belongings and their "children" as the boys attempted to fight off the enemy. All the situations the children

FUN WAS IMPORTANT TO CHEYENNE
ADULTS, TOO. HERE, MEN AND
WOMEN PLAY WINTER GAMES.

would encounter when they became adults were carefully rehearsed in their play.

The boys' first real hunts and war parties came early in their lives, when they were twelve or thirteen. A boy's first buffalo kill was an occasion for much celebration and honor. On the boys' first *warpath,* things were made easy for them, but they were not held back from taking an active part in the fight if they wished to do so. One Cheyenne, Crow Bed, told a historian the advice given him by his grandfather when Crow Bed, as a boy, set out on his first war party.

"Now," said the old warrior, "when the party is about to make a charge on the enemy, do not be afraid. When you fight, try to kill. Do not fear anything. It is not a disgrace to be killed in a fight."

THE SOCIAL ORGANIZATION OF THE TRIBE

Family and marriage were very important to the Cheyenne. The *courting* of a young woman by a young man was a bashful, long-drawn-out affair. In fact, when the boy finally popped the question of marriage, usually after four or five years of courtship, it was not considered good manners for him to do it himself. One of his relatives, usually an elderly female, went to the family of the girl and did the job for him. Family life was considered too important to leave to the impulses of young lovers.

But there was romance, too. Playing a medicine flute was believed to be a good means of casting a love spell over a reluctant girl. And certain medicine men could concoct a spruce gum that might do the trick for the eager young man. If the boy could get the girl to chew the gum, tradition had it that her thoughts could never

THIS DRAMATIC PAINTING, ENTITLED *INDIAN ELOPEMENT,* SHOWS HOW IMPORTANT MATTERS OF THE HEART WERE TO THE CHEYENNE.

stray far from him. If the family of the boy was pleased with his choice, they lavished gifts on the family of the girl, such as clothing, blankets, guns, bows and arrows, and horses. If the girl's family decided against the marriage, the gifts were returned. But if all went well, the girl was carried by the groom's relatives and friends into the tipi of the groom's family and set down in a place of honor. There her new female in-laws dressed her in clothes they had made for the festive occasion. They re-did her hair and repainted her. A feast followed, and soon afterward the newlyweds moved into a new tipi of their own. The tribe had gained a new family.

The Cheyenne tribe was divided into ten main *bands*. Four chiefs from each band, plus four principal chiefs, made up what was called the Council of Forty-four. This elected group was the governing body of the Cheyenne tribe. The council was represented by a set of four arrows, each a different color. These arrows, looked upon as sacred, symbolized the existence of the tribe.

The tribe was also broken down into military groups such as the Fox, Shield, Dog, and Bowstring. When a boy was ready to go to war, he sought to join one of these groups. The Bowstrings, also called the Contraries, were a small, very strange group—they did everything backward. Ask a Contrary to do one thing, and he would do another. A Contrary lived alone, apart from the rest of the people. He never married. He was given a sacred Contrary Bow, which was like a lance, but was

MILITARY SOCIETIES
WERE FORMED ON
THE BASIS OF
COMMON INTERESTS
AND WAR RITUALS.
THESE BLACK-AND-
WHITE PHOTOS SHOW
THE CHEYENNE LANCE
SOCIETY (ABOVE) AND
TWO SUN DANCE
PLEDGERS (LEFT).

SINCE THE MAN'S SHIRT ABOVE HAS SCALPS ATTACHED TO IT, IT WAS PROBABLY A WAR SHIRT.

THE WOMAN'S DEERSKIN DRESS AT LEFT WAS DECORATED TO MAKE IT MORE ATTRACTIVE.

not a weapon. It was carried into battle, but not for killing. Armed with his lance, the Contrary would often charge the enemy alone. Contraries were brave to the point of suicide, and were often followed as leaders in battle. When a Cheyenne dreamed he must become a Contrary, it was a great burden, but one of responsibility and sacredness.

The Cheyenne women had only one organization, the Quillers' Society, a select group. They created, or supervised, the embroidery of clothing with quills (sometimes from bird feathers, but most often from porcupines). The work of the Quillers was an important ceremony, surrounded by ritual.

SPIRITUAL BELIEFS

The Cheyenne as a group had various beliefs about what lay beyond the physical world that they could see, feel, smell, touch, and hear. There was a great deal of variety, however, in the beliefs of individuals. Some believed firmly in spirits and in the explanations of the universe that were the formal tribal answers to the mysteries of life. Other men and women had doubts about what they were told.

The Cheyenne believed in a two-part universe—one above the ground, one below—each ruled by a caring, merciful god. The god above was considered the Chief, the Creator, and he was called *Heammawihio,* the Wise One Above. The god below was *Ahktunowihio,* the Wise One Below. They also believed in four lesser, although powerful, spirits that dwelled at the four points of the compass.

The dead, it was believed, followed the "Hanging Road" above (the Milky Way), to where Heammawihio lived. Everyone who died went to him, it was believed, whether they were brave, cowardly, good, or bad. It was felt that all who died were equal, and that in the afterlife there was no punishment for sin nor reward for virtue. Above, the dead lived as they had on earth: hunting, going to war, and carrying on domestic duties.

Spirits were an important part of the Cheyenne religious beliefs. These spirits could appear as the sun, the moon, or as animals such as the badger that digs into the earth or the bear that lives in caves. They could take the form of human beings—an old man or woman or a handsome warrior or beautiful maiden. The Cheyenne did not fear these spirits, but thought of them as generous toward mankind. The spirits were also considered to be teachers from whom the Cheyenne could learn.

Many of the ceremonies of the Cheyenne sprang from their beliefs. The sacred arrows mentioned in the previous chapter were renewed in a solemn ceremony every few years. New feathers might be attached or the shafts of the arrows might be repainted. Known as the Renewal of the Sacred Arrow, the ceremony lasted four days, with dancing, songs, prayers, and many rituals. It was believed that these four arrows, which represented the soul of the tribe, had come from the gods, passed down through a legendary hero called Sweet Medicine.

Another important ceremony was the Sun Dance,

which celebrated the renewal of the earth. It lasted eight days. During the first four days a dance lodge was built; the last four days were given over to dancing. Families exchanged gifts, and there was much fun and laughter. Another tribal custom was the Animal Dance, performed to ensure successful hunting. An important symbol was the Sacred Buffalo Hat, or Medicine Hat. It was made of buffalo fur, with horns attached, and was

NOTE THAT IN THIS PAINTING OF THE DANCE OF THE SOLDIER SOCIETIES, SEVERAL THINGS SEEM TO BE OCCURRING AT THE SAME TIME.

IN THIS PAINTING DEPICTING THE
CHEYENNE CUSTOM OF LAYING THE DEAD TO
REST, THE LIFE AFTER DEATH IS SHOWN
IN THE TOP HALF OF THE PAINTING.
THE DEAD TRIBESMEMBER AND A HORSE
FOLLOW A PATH TO THEIR NEW HOME IN
THE AFTERLIFE WHERE HEAMMAWIHIO LIVED.

thought to have the power to ward off disease and turn away arrows and bullets in battle.

For healing, the Cheyenne looked to *medicine men,* combination doctors and priests, who were trained in the use of medicinal plants. These men were also skilled at setting bones, removing arrows, and stopping the flow of blood from wounds and other injuries. A healer was usually assisted by his wife or some other woman. In addition to medicinal herbs, healers used songs and prayers. Sometimes a healer would shake a rattle over the part of the patient's body that he felt was the source of the disease, or he would try to suck out the cause of the illness. Sometimes he used the wing of a hawk or eagle to fan the sick person. Sometimes he smoked a special stone pipe over the patient. Sometimes, if the patient desired, the patient himself was allowed to puff on the pipe. The medicine man was thought to be a mystic who bridged the gap between the physical world and the unseen worlds.

If the medicine man's healing arts failed and the patient died, the patient was dressed in his best clothes, wrapped in robes, and placed either on a scaffold, in a tree, or on the ground, and covered with rocks. With him were placed his weapons, tools, and other things that he might need in the afterlife. Sometimes his favorite horse was killed for his use. Then the dead man was ready to meet the Wise One Above.

WAR WITH THE UNITED STATES

During the early nineteenth century, when the Western plains were visited only by traders, explorers, and occasional travelers, the Cheyenne had no serious quarrel with white people. In fact, in the early part of the century the white public considered the Indians of the West to be the most romantic of peoples. Many whites, some of them rich and famous, came from the East and from Europe to ride with the Indians, to eat roast buffalo ribs, and to study the great hunters. But in the 1840s, relations with the whites began to take a turn for the worse.

White settlers were heading in great numbers across Indian territory to the West. As they moved westward, they brought with them diseases such as *cholera*, against which the Indians had no *immunity*. In one summer, nearly half of the Cheyenne tribe was wiped out by that dreadful disease. In 1849, gold was discovered in California, and some twenty thousand fortune hunters flocked through Cheyenne country on their way to the West Coast. The Indian tribes, which had often fought against each other, now began to band together against the white settlers. For the Cheyenne, the war began in earnest in 1856. A small group of Cheyenne warriors, part of a large war party that was doing battle against the Pawnee tribe, frightened the driver of a mail coach, who fired on them. In return, he received an arrow wound. The next day, a troop of the U.S. *Cavalry* attacked a Cheyenne camp, killing eighteen people. The Cheyenne retaliated by attacking two wagon trains, killing a high U.S. official and six other men, women, and children. Whites and Indians began killing each other without discrimination. If an Indian band made an attack on settlers, U.S. soldiers killed Indians, whether those particular Indians were guilty or not. The Indians followed suit, falling on innocent pioneers. Attempts to mediate had little success. Treaties were ignored—usually by the whites—when it was convenient to do so.

Many whites sympathized with the Indians, who were being pushed off their lands. Other whites subscribed to a catch phrase of the day: "The only good Indian is a dead Indian." One of the latter was a Colonel John M. Chivington, who with seven hundred vol-

A CHEYENNE ENCAMPMENT IS SURPRISED BY
AN ATTACK OF U.S. SOLDIERS AT DAWN.

unteers of the Colorado Militia attacked a peaceful Cheyenne camp in 1864. An American flag raised by the Cheyenne chief, Black Kettle, provided no mercy. The surprised and bewildered Cheyenne fought back bitterly, but they were overwhelmed. Women and children were slaughtered by the soldiers. Over two hundred Cheyenne died that day. Their bodies were savagely mutilated by drunken soldiers. Scalps and severed arms and legs were taken to Denver and displayed in a theater.

A wide protest broke out among the white population. The famed frontiersman Kit Carson called the soldiers "cowards and dogs." The U.S. Congress forced Colonel Chivington to resign from the Army. But the damage had been done. During the following years, hundreds of white settlers were killed by Indians, and their women and children taken into captivity. Thousands of the settlers' cattle and horses were set free. Wagon trains, trading posts, and stagecoach stations were looted and burned.

At this time, the U.S. Army was fighting the Civil War in the East. The few troops stationed in the West could not cope with the tension between the whites and the Indians. When the Civil War ended in 1865, the military was free to unleash its full force on the Indians. There was little hope for the five thousand Cheyenne, twenty thousand Sioux, and a few thousand each of Arapaho, Comanche, Crow, Ute, and others to carry on a defensive war with success.

One of the most publicized Army figures of the time was Colonel George A. Custer. He was a blond, long-haired young officer. The Indians called him Yellow Hair. He had first come to wide public attention in 1868 when he led an Army attack on a Cheyenne village. Some sixty braves and many women and children were killed in the attack. Soon after, nineteen Cheyenne chiefs offered total surrender; their people had no resources with which to carry on against the overwhelming numbers of the U.S. Army. But the band of Cheyenne Dog Soldiers refused to capitulate. They drifted northward to Kansas and joined with a band of Sioux who had also refused to give up. These resisters numbered some five hundred warriors and their families. They chose to fight to the finish.

During the next few years, this group continued their desperate action against the whites. But in 1876, they had one great moment of revenge. It was at the expense of Custer, which made it all the more sweet. This moment is called the Battle of Little Bighorn.

The glory-seeking Custer had attempted a foolish, reckless attack on a huge encampment of Sioux and Cheyenne. Custer was commanding the elite Seventh Cavalry, organized for the specific purpose of finally conquering the Indians of the Plains. Custer's command was destroyed to a man; 264 soldiers died with him. For the U.S. Army, it was a humiliating defeat. A modern nation of 40 million people had been beaten by what

GEORGE A. CUSTER HAD BEEN SUSPENDED FOR
TEN MONTHS FROM THE U.S. ARMY, BUT WAS
RESTORED TO ACTIVE DUTY FOR A CAMPAIGN
AGAINST THE INDIANS. AFTER THE BATTLE
OF LITTLE BIGHORN, HE WAS ACCUSED OF
HAVING BEEN "RECKLESS" WITH HIS MEN.

CUSTER'S LAST STAND—WHERE CHEYENNE
SOLDIERS ROUTED U.S. TROOPS AT THE
BATTLE OF LITTLE BIGHORN

CRAZY HORSE (LEFT) AND SITTING BULL
WERE TWO OF THE CHIEFS WHO LED THE
CHEYENNE, SIOUX, OGLALA, AND MINICONJOU
IN THE BATTLE OF LITTLE BIGHORN.

many had considered just a few savages. And the humiliation occurred at the height of the 100th anniversary celebration of the formation of the United States.

It was a glorious victory for the Cheyenne and Sioux, under such famous leaders as Sitting Bull and Crazy Horse, but a costly one as well. The Plains were now swarming with U.S. troops, eager for revenge. The Indians had little time to savor their triumph. They were forced to break up into small groups and scatter. The soldiers harassed them unmercifully, and within two years of the Indians' greatest success the Cheyenne gave up and surrendered. The U.S. government grouped the Cheyenne with the Arapaho and sent them to a reservation in what is now Oklahoma.

THE VALIANT FLIGHT

For many years, the Cheyenne had been divided into two groups, the Northern Cheyenne and the Southern Cheyenne. The U.S. government had come to deal with each group separately, and the Cheyenne thought of themselves as two separate branches of the same original tribe. After the collapse of the Plains Indians' widespread resistance, the Northern Cheyenne were sent to the reservation of the Southern Cheyenne, in what is now Oklahoma. The Northerners were not happy there. They were not used to the summer heat of this land, and there was little game and poor shelter. The U.S. government's Indian Bureau did not send the food and supplies that had been promised. *Malaria,* a disease of warm climates, swept through the Northerners' ranks. And most difficult of all to endure, they were homesick for their familiar land, 1,500 miles (2,414 km) to the north.

In 1878, under the leadership of two chiefs, Dull Knife and Little Wolf, about three hundred Northern Cheyenne slipped through the guard of soldiers that surrounded them. They headed north for their homeland. Only about seventy were warriors, the rest were women, children, and old people. The Cheyenne skillfully hid their trail. It was six weeks before they were finally caught, even though a force of about thirteen thousand soldiers pursued them. They turned to fight when the troops caught up with them.

The route they covered was no longer empty land; it now teemed with white settlers. The escaping Cheyenne tried to avoid contact with whites, but they needed horses and meat, and there were no other sources than the horses and cattle of the pioneers. There were exchanges of gunfire, and some settlers were killed. The Indians' route, which crossed three railroads—the Atchison, Topeka & Santa Fe; the Kansas Pacific; and the Union Pacific—were all heavily guarded by U.S. troops. But the Cheyenne used shrewd strategies and slipped through. At one point, they muffled the hooves of their horses and maneuvered their way by night between two troops of U.S. Cavalry. In the morning, the only sign of the Indians was the footprints of their horses.

By this time, the eyes of the United States, and the world, were on this gallant, seemingly impossible, flight for freedom. Many people called for the Indians' de-

CHIEFS LITTLE WOLF AND DULL KNIFE TRIED TO LEAD THEIR PEOPLE TO THEIR HOMELAND IN MONTANA. ALAS, THE GROUP LED BY LITTLE WOLF WOULD HAVE A FAR BETTER EXPERIENCE THAN THE GROUP LED BY DULL KNIFE.

CHEYENNE INDIANS TRAVELING TO THEIR RESERVATION

struction, but many others cheered the Indians on. When the last railroad line was crossed, the Cheyenne broke up into two groups, one under each chief. The group led by Little Wolf continued northward toward the Black Hills of South Dakota. They were able to hide and settle down for the winter, and in the spring they continued their journey. They met with U.S. soldiers who were sympathetic to them. They surrendered, since they had reached Montana, their goal. They were well treated, and the story for this band has a relatively happy ending.

Not so for the group under Dull Knife. They had progressed almost to Montana when, in a blinding snowstorm, they ran into two companies of U.S. Cavalry. Exhausted, sick, and surrounded by overwhelming military force, they agreed to accompany the troops to Camp Robinson, in the northwestern corner of North Dakota. They surrendered their weapons under pressure, but gave up only their oldest rifles—the best ones were secretly taken apart and hidden under the women's clothing. The group was quartered in an empty barracks and at first was treated with kindness. They knew, however, that at any moment someone in Washington might make a decision to send them back to the southern reservation from which they had fled.

By this time, this small band of refugees had become a focus of world attention. Hard times were coming. The temperature dropped lower and lower, as low as 40° F below zero (−40° C). Word came from Washington that the group was to be sent south. The Cheyenne told their captors they would rather die than go back. They were given no more food or firewood. Even their water supply was withheld.

The Cheyenne braves reassembled the rifles they had hidden, and armed themselves with kitchen knives. One frigid night, warriors of the Dog Society leaped through the windows of the barracks and shot the *sentries*. The Cheyenne men, women, and children poured from the barracks and struggled to bluffs 2 miles (3 km) distant, fighting all the way. When Cheyenne warriors fell, the women and young boys picked up the guns and fought. Many Cheyenne were killed or wounded, but others were able to push on, hungry and weak, through the bitter cold and snow. Some were crippled with frostbite. Some carried children and wounded. Repeatedly, they fought their way free of the pursuing soldiers. At last, twelve days after the break-out, the end came. The Cheyenne were surrounded, and the air was filled with their death chants. As the soldiers fired on the Cheyenne, three warriors charged the white troops. They were quickly shot down. It was three against three hundred.

Seven male Cheyenne who seemed well enough to stand trial were taken to Kansas. Defense funds poured in from all over the country; lawyers offered their services without cost. The case was dismissed, and the Indian Bureau forced the survivors to go south temporarily. However, public indignation forced the officials in Washington to back down. The few Northern Cheyenne who remained were allowed to go north to Montana, their home. They had paid a heavy price, but in the eyes of the world they had outwitted and outfought a military force that outnumbered them more than one hundred to one. They had made their mark on history.

THE CHEYENNE TODAY

The lot of the Cheyenne today, like that of most Native Americans, is not an enviable one. About three thousand Northern Cheyenne live on their reservation at Lame Deer, Montana, and about five thousand Southern Cheyenne cluster in towns near the tribal headquarters at Concho, Oklahoma. Living in the white world has never been easy for the Indian. Unemployment among Indians is very high. In looking for jobs off the reservation, Indians often have strikes against them just because they are not white. And Indians as a group do not tend to seek the education that will get them high-paying jobs. There is a mixed feeling toward education; many Indians feel that trying to climb the ladder in the white civilization is somehow betraying their own culture.

Alcoholism has long been a major problem with

Indians. Destruction of their way of life often has led to a feeling of helplessness and depression. Many of today's young Indians have problems with drugs.

One Southern Cheyenne woman, Rose Sleeper, reports: "There is a real prejudice here in Oklahoma. Some white police are after the Indian. Some teachers are prejudiced against us. The Indian has two faces, one for the Indian and one for the white. With the white, we are more formal; with the Indian, we laugh and are humorous. Although I've met white people who are real fun. Some have really cracked me up."

Barbara Spang, who lives on the Northern Cheyenne reservation and is a great-granddaughter of Chief Dull Knife, feared that the Cheyenne language was dying out. "Most young people don't speak Cheyenne anymore. In another fifty years our language may not exist," she said sadly.

But some people are fighting to reverse this trend. One is Lucille Youngblood of the Southern Cheyenne. Ms. Youngblood, whose Indian name is White Buffalo Woman (most Cheyenne have both a white name and an Indian name), is now working hard to teach the Cheyenne language to young people. She feels there has been a revival of Indian culture in recent years. "We do powwows," she said, "and Indian dances and songs. The Cheyenne legends are still handed down to the children."

(ABOVE) A FAMILY POSES FOR A PHOTOGRAPH ON
THE CHEYENNE RESERVATION IN MONTANA.
(RIGHT) A WIDOW COMFORTS HER SON AT
THE ONE-YEAR ANNIVERSARY
SERVICE OF HER HUSBAND'S DEATH.

SOME ASPECTS OF CHEYENNE LIFE REMAIN AS THEY
HAVE ALWAYS BEEN: (ABOVE) TWO FULL-BLOODED
CHEYENNE BROTHERS GOURD DANCE AT A POWWOW
AT THE ST. LABRE INDIAN SCHOOL ON
THE CHEYENNE RESERVATION IN MONTANA,
AND (AT RIGHT) A BOY USES A LASSO
TO ROUND UP HORSES.

White Buffalo Woman feels that after the conquest of the Indians, white Americans tried to make Indians into white people. They were sent to schools and given white educations. Churches moved in and tried to eradicate the Indian religions and prevent Indians from speaking their own languages. But there has been something of a reversal of this trend in the past two or three decades, she feels, possibly because of the Civil Rights movement. "We have sun dances," she says, "and we have a sacred tipi now." But, she says, "It's hard for an Indian to live in this culture."

Rose Sleeper recalls an incident from her childhood. "My mother was driving along with us kids, and as we went by some white kids they put their hands on their mouths and went 'Woo-woo!' My mother stopped the car and went back to them, and she told them that this land belonged to us before it was taken by the white man. They got real quiet."

GLOSSARY

Ahktunowihio The god who, the Cheyenne believed, ruled below the earth; the "Great One Below."

Antelope A fleet-footed, deerlike wild animal.

Buffalo An oxlike animal—more correctly called the bison—once common in the western United States. It was hunted almost to extinction.

Cavalry Soldiers trained to fight on horseback.

Cholera A diarrheal disease that easily spreads among many people; can be deadly if not treated.

Colt A young horse.

Courting Paying attention to another person, often to gain love.

Game Play, or a contest; also, wild animals that are hunted.

Graze An animal's feeding on growing grass.

Heammawihio The Cheyenne word for God; the Creator, or "Great One Above."

Immunity Protection from a disease because of having been previously exposed to it.

La Salle, Sieur de A French explorer who lived from 1643 to 1687.

Lasso A long line of rope, made from animal hide, with a running noose, used for catching horses or cattle.

Lodge A dwelling place.

Malaria A disease caused by the bite of certain types of mosquitoes.

Medicine man A member of the tribe who used herbs and other means to cure illnesses and injuries, and protect against evil spirits.

Nomads A wandering group of people.

Prairie Level or rolling treeless land common to the western United States.

Prickly pear A type of cactus that contains a pear-shaped fruit.

Sentries Watchers or guards.

Spanish conquistadores Spanish soldiers sent to conquer native peoples in North and South America.

Tipi (sometimes spelled teepee) A cone-shaped Indian dwelling made of skins of animals or cloth.

Tsistsistas A Cheyenne word for their tribe, meaning "the beautiful people."

Warpath When Indians went out to do battle.

FOR FURTHER READING

Curtis, Natalie. *The Indians' Book—Songs and Legends of the American Indians*. New York: Dover Publications, 1968.

Fradin, Dennis B. *The Cheyenne*. Chicago: Childrens Press, 1988.

Tall Bull, Henry, and Weist, Tom. *Cheyenne Legends of Creation*. Billings, Montana: Council for Indian Education, 1972.

Tall Bull, Henry, and Weist, Tom. *Cheyenne Warriors*. Billings, Montana: Council for Indian Education, 1976.

Hoig, Stanley. *The Cheyenne*. New York: Chelsea House, 1989.

Josephy, Alvin (Editor). *The American Heritage Book of*

Indians. Washington, D.C.: American Heritage Publications Co., 1961.

Sandoz, Mari. *Cheyenne Autumn*. New York: Hastings House, 1953.

Stands in Timber, John, and Liberty, Margot. *Cheyenne Memories*. New Haven: Yale University Press, 1988.

A good way to become aware of the problems of the Cheyenne today is to see a feature film released in 1989 called *Powwow Highway*. Using Indian actors, the film, which begins on the Northern Cheyenne reservation at Lame Deer, Montana, tells of the effort of one young Cheyenne man to recapture the pride of the tribesmen of days gone by. It was produced by Handmade Films of Los Angeles, and is available on video.

INDEX

ABOUT THE AUTHOR

Arthur Myers has been a newspaper and magazine writer and editor and has published a number of books, several of them for children. He lives in Wellesley, Massachusetts.